A PILGRIMAGE THROUGH GRIEF

A PILGRIMAGE THROUGH GRIEF

Healing the Soul's Hurt After Loss

Text and photographs by
James E. Miller

Abbey Press
St. Meinrad, IN 47577

© 1995 by James E. Miller
Published by One Caring Place
Abbey Press
St. Meinrad, Indiana 47577

Library of Congress Catalog Number
95-70405

ISBN 0-87029-291-9

Book design by Scott Wannemuehler

Manufactured in China

To Christen,
both daughter and friend,
both loved and loving.

Contents

Acknowledgments. ix

Foreword. xi

Introduction—A Strange Land. 1

An Invitation to Be a Pilgrim. 11

The Experience of Absence. 21

The Experience of Aloneness. 35

The Experience of Silence. 51

The Experience of Mystery. 63

The Return. 77

Acknowledgments

This book began four years ago as an audiovisual presentation entitled *By the Waters of Babylon: A Spiritual Pilgrimage for a Time of Dislocation.* Little did I know when I conceived the idea for its theme, as I prepared to introduce it at a large national conference, that I would be creating it during a personal time of dislocation. My wife, Bernie, developed breast cancer and underwent surgery and chemotherapy during the months these words were first written. The words come, therefore, directly from the soul.

While this is in many ways a very personal creation, three people added their influence by offering critical feedback along the way: Clare Barton, Jennifer Levine, and Bernie herself. Without their thoughtful input, my writing, not to mention my life, would have been more muddied.

This book has taken the form in which it now appears through the influence of three people from Abbey Press: Linus Mundy, who first believed in the project and made it happen; Lisa Engelhardt, who moved over the words with a touch that was both light and knowing; and Scott Wannemuehler, who gave this piece its distinctive design.

But in reality many, many others have made this book possible: parishioners and counselees who opened their lives to me, friends and colleagues through the years who opened their hearts and minds and souls, and those especially dear ones who have been close beside me on this journey of my life.

—*James E. Miller*
August 28, 1995

Foreword

Isn't it strange how you can know someone long before you've met that person? I first came to know Jim Miller through the photographic beauty and poetic prose of two of his videos, *Invincible Summer* and *How Do I Go On?* As I watched those videos, tears flowed down my face. I wondered, *Who is this man, and how has he come to know so deeply the pain and promise of loss and grief?*

By the time I was introduced to *A Pilgimage Through Grief,* I knew Jim as a tried-and-true friend. He listened to my anguish when my mother was diagnosed with lung cancer. He phoned me almost daily as I cared for her, and he drove a great distance so he could be with me when she died.

The Jim Miller I have come to know as friend is the same one you will meet in these pages. He is one of the most constant, compassionate, and deeply spiritual people I know. He is also outrageous. With the gentlest words imaginable, he invites us to take up the losses of our lives and journey with them over sacred ground. He does not dwell on how shaky that ground will feel to the pilgrim beginning the journey, nor does he deny it. He simply calls us onward.

He is unwavering in his persuasion. Although we may feel

helpless and lethargic, he tells us there are choices we can make. With confidence he shows us how we can embrace our loneliness and befriend the absence. He promises that in listening to silence we will hear a voice—not a stranger's voice, but one who knows our name. *Come,* he implores. *Darkness will yield to insight and wisdom. It will lead us home to ourselves.*

As outrageous and paradoxical as Jim's call to pilgrimage seems, it reflects my own experiences of loss and grief. This is the journey I took over and over again during the many years of my son's illness. It is the familiar ground I walked after he died. It is the paradox I have encountered in my counseling practice. It is the message underlying countless stories I have heard as I have traveled around the world.

I will tell you of one such experience. Several years ago, I was invited to participate in a weekend camp for grieving children. The children were in one part of the campsite; their parents were in another. My role was to plan and orchestrate the parents' camp. The group included eighteen adults whose children or spouses had recently died—some from sudden accidents and random violence, others from long and arduous illness. We came as strangers to tell our stories and to garner whatever hope we could that life might once again hold promise and vitality.

We had only three days to embrace ourselves, our absent

loved ones, and each other. Some, whose losses were raw, whose energy was exhausted, were almost frozen in their paths. One-by-cautious-one, these people spoke, stumbling over their words, groping through their dark emotions. In time that could not be measured by hours, we knew something was happening. Both words and tears combined into our hearts' healing flow.

How did this happen? We were broken and yet whole. The pain of the other was impenetrable and yet we were inside it. The journey was ineffably singular and yet we were not alone. The experience was, like this book, outrageous. It defied words and yet words were the vehicle. It was awful and awe-full.

As I sat in that circle of people where pain was raging and raw, all theory and book knowledge seemed empty and trite. I knew I must stay centered in the truth I had learned from my own life's journey: Pain is also promise. Grief can lead to growth. We are not alone but are companioned by a Presence that calls us home to our deepest selves.

In this book, Jim Miller gives to each of us a harbor of hope, an undeniable promise from one who has journeyed before us. We can lean on his unwavering convictions as we take the first tenuous step on our pilgrimage through grief.

—Donna O'Toole
Founder and director of Rainbow Connection, resources
and training to help people grow through loss and change

A Strange Land

By the rivers of Babylon—
   there we sat down and there we wept
     when we remembered Zion.
On the willows there
   we hung up our harps.
For there our captors asked us for songs,
   and our tormentors asked for mirth, saying,
     "Sing us one of the songs of Zion!"
How could we sing the Lord's song in a foreign land?
                    —Psalm 137:1-4

*T*he experience to which these words refer
    is as old as 2500 years
        and as new as today.
It is the story of what happens to us
    when life places us somewhere we don't want to be.
So it was for the Israelites.
They were forcibly marched to Babylon,
    the land of their enemies,
        after being defeated in war.
Torn from their homes,
    separated from those they loved,
        they were made to live in surroundings that felt strange.
They did not know how long this exile would last.
It could be years at least,
    and maybe an entire generation, if not a whole lifetime.
So when their captors asked them to sing their native songs,
    their hymns of happiness,
        the Israelites declined.
For how could they possibly sing the Lord's song
    in a place so foreign?

*T*his is an experience many of *us* know as well.
We may have been placed somewhere we don't want to be.
We may have had to give up something or someone
   we didn't want to give up.
We may have lost what it hurt to lose.
Whatever happened,
   we may have found ourselves in a strange place,
      missing desperately who or what is no longer with us,
         and surrounded by those who may not understand.
And we may be wondering,
   "How could we sing the Lord's song
      in a place that feels so uncomfortable?"

"*H*ow *can* we sing the Lord's song in this foreign land?"
There is no easy answer to our question.
There are only answers that come from living
    while feeling as if we are dying within.
Only answers that recognize that each of us is unique.
Only answers that accept that each of us must find our own way.
There is help, of course.
There are people who have gone before,
    and they have much to teach us.
There are people in similar situations around us,
    and together we have much worth sharing.
Still, the question posed is a personal one.
And so must be the answer.

*L*ife-changing events affect every part of us:
    our mind, our heart, our body, our soul.
Each part is important.
But the part we intend to address here is the soul.
Our purpose here
    is to connect with the spiritual side of ourselves
        and to become aware of the part our soul plays
            in all that happens to us,
                today and tomorrow.
This time when we feel dislocated and unsettled
    is a critical time for us.
It calls into question
    who we have been and what we have done,
        who we are and what we are doing today,
            who we can be and what life will be like for us tomorrow.
Change is in the air.
But *how* shall we change?
And *what* shall we change?
And what shall we *keep*?
How can we make this important time of change
    as much as possible a time of *growth*?
What can we do to encourage genuine growth within us
    and healing presence around us?

An Invitation to Be a Pilgrim

All of us are pilgrims on this earth.
I have even heard people say
  that the earth itself is a pilgrim
    in the heavens.

—Maxim Gorky

We can be in touch with our spiritual selves in many ways.
The way we're exploring here is based
   on an age-old spiritual discipline—
      the act of going on a pilgrimage.
The act of taking a journey,
   and visiting one or more places
      that hold a certain significance for us,
         and after awhile returning home,
            enlightened by that journey.
Pilgrimages have played a role in every major religion.
Pilgrims have walked every continent,
   visited almost every mountain and desert,
      meditated at every major religious site,
         and many minor ones.
We join a long and honored tradition.

If any student of this art
is afraid of hard work,
let him stop with his foot
upon the threshold.

—Philalethes

A pilgrimage is not a lark.
It is a journey that requires effort, even sacrifice.
It can be a lonely experience,
    because by definition a pilgrimage is an individual endeavor.
Others may travel alongside,
    but each pilgrim is making his own personal journey;
      each has her own itinerary.
A pilgrimage is something we cannot hurry,
    else it stops being a pilgrimage.
We stop and start and stop again,
    because one of our goals is to be in touch with the sacred,
      and that does not easily happen on a rigid schedule,
        nor does it happen quickly.
And a pilgrimage is always a round trip.
We leave home in order to return home.
We go away in order to see and to meditate and to learn,
    so that we can come back somehow different,
      somehow broadened,
        somehow better for what has happened to us.

*T*his book is intended as a call to pilgrimage
and as a guide along the way.
It is an invitation for each of us to take our own pilgrimage—
a pilgrimage not of geography, but of personal experience,
not of the body, but of the soul,
not where others have always led,
but where we have already been
and where we are already going.
The possibilities are many.
We'll suggest here just four experiences:
the experience of absence,
the experience of aloneness,
the experience of silence,
and the experience of mystery.

May those who sow in tears
   reap with shouts of joy.
Those who go out weeping,
   bearing the seed for sowing,
      shall come home with shouts of joy,
         carrying their sheaves.

—Psalm 126:5, 6

*T*hese words were originally composed for pilgrims
 on their way to Jerusalem.
They express the hope that *all* pilgrims carry,
 that even *we* carry today.
Because of what has happened to us, we may go forth weeping.
We go forth missing what we have lost,
 grieving for what we may never have.
Yet we go forth knowing that on pilgrimage
 there are sights for us to see,
 and lessons for us to absorb,
 and secrets for us to uncover.
We set forth believing something important is in store for us,
 and yearning to make it ours.
We begin our journey of the spirit
 prepared for the greatest pilgrimage of all—
 the one that goes deep within in search of who we are,
 and ready to discover who, and Whose, we might be.

The Experience of Absence

My eyes fill with tears.
What shall I do?
Where shall I go?
Who can quench my pain?
My body has been bitten
By the snake of "absence,"
And my life is ebbing away
With every beat of the heart.

—Mirabai

*T*he words composed by this fifteenth-century Indian poet
   reach across years and continents to touch us.
We, too, can be stung by absence.
We, too, can be plagued by emptiness.
What we had is gone.
What we took for granted is missing.
What we presumed would be will not come to be.
Around us we feel only barrenness.
And the poet's questions from another era
   become our questions today.
"Where shall I go?"
"What shall I do?"
Even more difficult,
   "Why must I face this absence, this emptiness?"
Whether it is the absence of meaning or of hope,
   the absence of someone we have loved
      or of something we have held dear,
         the question "Why?" surfaces ever so easily.

*T*he emptiness around us reminds us of that other emptiness:
 the one within.
Both ask for some sort of response.
Both call for something to be done.
It may well be our best response is the simplest
 and the most difficult: acceptance.
We must accept the absence.
We must feel the wideness by our side,
 the openness that stretches out all around us,
 the hollowness within.
And we must let that absence be.
We must allow it time.
Rather than push the absence away, as we all want to do,
 we will do well to draw it near.
We will do well to befriend it,
 asking of it not questions that demand
 but queries that may open possibilities.
"What does this emptiness most want to say to me?"
"What does this absence have to teach me?"
"What is there in this uninterrupted expanse
 that wants to interrupt me and expand my vision?"
"What am I being given the opportunity to learn
 about myself, about this world, about this life?"

Why have you forsaken me?
Why are you so far from helping me...?

—Psalm 22:1

*"Come away to a deserted place
all by yourselves and rest awhile."*

—Jesus of Nazareth, in Mark 6:31

*L*ike many spiritual leaders,
  Jesus of Nazareth knew the value of spending time
    in places without distractions.
His pattern, in fact, was to visit empty places regularly.
He, and many others, knew what the results can be.
Barrenness focuses our attention.
It helps us see what we might otherwise miss.
It helps us isolate what really matters.

*T*here's more.
Remote places can surprise us with their unexpected beauty.
If we wait, and watch, and look,
    (with our souls as much as with our eyes)
        a gift will be given us:
            the gift of truly seeing.
And in time, somehow, paradoxically,
    in these places that seem most depleted
        we can begin to experience a richness.
In these spaces where there seems to be so little,
    we can begin to find enough,
        and even more than enough.

*A*nd the greatest paradox is this:
When we immerse ourselves in absence,
    something other can be revealed:
A presence.
Not just a presence, but a Presence.
Beyond words, beyond even understanding,
    we are somehow touched.
We are somehow held in connection.
We are somehow awakened.
We can begin to see that behind the randomness
    that seems to rule our life,
        there is an essential order.
Beneath the simplicity we see,
    there is a miraculous complexity and a wonderful harmony.
And beyond the emptiness we may experience,
    there is a fullness that waits for us,
        and calls to us,
            and reaches for us.
All we need do to respond is to speak one unspoken word:
    "Yes."

*M*ay your time of emptiness come also to be a time
when you begin to see what you have not seen before,
when you begin to experience
something you have been missing.
May you find it within yourself
to be able to speak one unspoken word.
And may that word be "Yes."

The Experience
of Aloneness

There is no one who takes notice of me;
   no refuge remains to me,
      no one cares for me.

—Psalm 142:4

I am like a lonely bird on the housetop.

—Psalm 102:7

When change invades our life against our will,
   or when we must let go against our desires,
      something can happen to our feelings about ourselves.
Before, we felt support around us.
Now, we feel vulnerable and exposed.
Before, we felt we were in company.
Now, we may feel solitary and alone.
Our feelings run deep.
Our questions may run even deeper:
"Who *am* I, who feels so alone?"
"Why must I feel this way?"
"What is to become of me?"
"What am I to do?"

The only true wisdom
   lies far from humankind,
      out in the great loneliness.
            —Eskimo saying

*T*here *is* wisdom that loneliness can hold for us.
But it is a wisdom that reveals itself only with time,
    and only by way of effort,
    and only through courage.
For facing the world alone is an arduous task,
    even a frightening one.
But there is a decision here we *can* make,
    a choice which *is* ours,
        a choice which no one else can make for us.
And the very act of making that decision is a major step
    in coming to grips with our solitariness.
That decision is to embrace our aloneness for what it is.
That decision is to let our loneliness
    surround us and envelop us,
        so we can become more familiar with it,
            so we can make it our own.
We have an opportunity which may not seem like one:
    the opportunity to face what is there—ourselves.
Only ourselves.

We can begin by unfolding ourselves,
   slowly and quietly.
By looking gently at those parts of ourselves
   we have long hidden.
By looking forgivingly at those parts of ourselves
   we have long regretted.
By looking lovingly at those parts
      that yearn to come to the light,
         and there perhaps to blossom.

*T*his is our chance to know ourselves
in a way we've never quite known ourselves before:
uncrowded, unprotected, unhurried.
What we'll find is what we're afraid to find:
that we're less than we wish,
that we're as imperfect as we feared.
But having faced that,
we'll discover something much more important:
that by laying open what we've been hiding,
and what we've been hiding from,
we set it loose.
We free it.
And at the same time it will free us.
It will loosen the grip it had on us—
a grip we barely recognized.
New energies will be released from within:
the creative part of us,
the part that wants to grow,
the part that is ready to reach beyond.

Something else happens.
By coming to understand ourselves better,
    we come to understand others better.
This is, in fact, the *only* way to understand those around us.
It seems contradictory but it is true:
    our aloneness makes possible our togetherness.
We discover that we are not the only ones who are alone.
We all are alone, and we all are together,
    sharing many of the same fears and longings,
        similar scars and similar dreams.
Seen this way—
    alone and yet together, together and yet alone—
        our understanding of who we are, and why we are here,
            can grow.
Our appreciation for what we have been given,
    and for what we have yet to give, will deepen.
And we can begin to see what we may have forgotten
    or what we may have submerged:
        that each of us is, indeed, a marvel.
Each of us is no less than a miracle.
Each of us has been given the most incomprehensible gift:
    this life.
All of us have been placed in the most unimaginable home:
    this earth.
We have been gifted with one another.

*T*here is another truth for us to learn.
Wherever we are in our aloneness, wherever we go,
    Another is always with us.
Whatever we do, and however we feel,
    Another is always there beside us.
And when we finally realize and accept
    that we are accompanied by this Supreme Other
        through every moment of our lives,
            a shift begins to take place.
Our loneliness becomes less a loneliness
    and more a solitude.
We feel less an anguish and more a comfort,
    less threat and more promise.
The promise is that by living fully our aloneness,
    we can become more whole.
We can become more who we are meant to be.
We can come to know
    what the prophet Isaiah meant
        when through him God said,
"I have called you by name, you are mine.
When you pass through the waters, I will be with you;
    and through the rivers, they shall not overwhelm you;
        when you walk through fire you shall not be burned....
For I am...the Holy One...your Savior."

—Isaiah 43:1-3

*M*ay your aloneness become more than your aloneness.
May it deepen you and broaden you.
May it awaken you and connect you.
May you come to know that you are always more than you.
And may you know that in a way you will never forget.

The Experience of Silence

*I cry by day, but you do not answer;
and by night, but find no rest.*

—Psalm 22:2

*S*ilence can be uncomfortable.
If we want an answer, and one does not come,
   we are disappointed.
If we wish to hear one particular voice,
   and that voice is silent,
      we feel discontented.
If we are used to sound all around us,
   and that sound disappears,
      we find ourselves at a loss.
Despite the adage, silence is not always golden.
It may be frustrating, even fearful.
It may remind us of what we have lost,
   or what we may yet lose.
It may tie us to a past we wish to forget,
   or to a future we would like to ignore.
Silence may link us to a present moment
   that feels too empty, too alone, too unknown.
Yet somehow we know,
   from what others have said,
      from what we have said to ourselves,
         that there is value in silence.

Every person who delights in a multitude of words,
   even though he says admirable things,
     is empty within.
If you love the truth, be a lover of silence.
It brings you a fruit that tongue cannot describe.

                   —St. Isaac of Ninevah

Silence is much more than the absence of sound
   and the dying away of words.
Silence has a presence all its own.
It is not empty, but full.
It harbors a richness, a wholeness.
It brims with meaning.

Silence communicates in its own unique way.
And what it communicates is often what we most need to hear.
It can lead us to see what we have too often missed.
The words of Psalm 19 describe what words cannot do:

> *The heavens are telling the glory of God;*
> *and the firmament proclaims his handiwork.*
> *Day to day pours forth speech,*
> *and night to night declares knowledge.*
> *There is no speech, nor are there words;*
> *their voice is not heard;*
> *yet their voice goes out through all the earth,*
> *and their words to the end of the world.*

—Psalm 19:1-4

The psalmist knows.
The heavens speak...in silence.
The earth talks...without words.
Morning proclaims...in quietude.
Evening preaches...without a syllable.
Trees declare, fields announce,
flowers make eloquent statements...
and not a sound is heard, not a sentence is formed.

*I*t can be likewise with us.
When we build a space for silence around us,
    when we give silence time to settle in and settle down,
        we will find that an inner voice awaits us there.
The sound of the Eternal is the sound of silence.
It barely whispers, yet it fills the air around us.
It saturates all that is, but it speaks as Silence to silence,
    its Silence to our silence.
And our silence responds.
Its Stillness calls to our stillness, and our stillness answers.
Deep inside, we come to know,
    far beyond what any sound can convey.
Deep within, we come to be assured,
    far beyond any verbal assurance.
In our quietness we come to be even more quieted,
    held within by the greatest Quiet of all.

*M*ay this time of your life be rich in its silences.
May you discover a stillness that supports you,
  and a calmness that anchors you.
May you hear the Voice that speaks ever so silently,
  ever so surely.
And may what you hear speak your name.

The Experience of Mystery

How long must I bear pain in my soul?
—Psalm 13:2

And now, O Lord, what do I wait for?
—Psalm 39:7

Why, O Lord, do you stand far off?
—Psalm 10:1

We don't like not knowing.
We don't like the experience
    of having our deeply felt questions go unanswered.
We have been trained to look for solutions
    and to expect responses.
Then those times in our lives come
    when questions multiply within.
Those times when our preconceptions have been broken,
    or when our expectations have been dashed,
        or when our anticipations have been denied.
We want "whys" and "wherefores"
    and often we find we cannot have them.
We want to know the "whens" and the "hows"
    and we are not given them.
We want to be introduced to the "whos":
    who am I and who art Thou?
Sometimes we barely know.

Be patient toward all that is unsolved in your heart
and try to love the questions themselves....
And the point is, to live everything.
Live the questions now.
Perhaps you will then gradually, without noticing it,
live along some distant day into the answer.

—Rainer Maria Rilke

When we are patient with our questions,
when we live them,
we will realize that questions are always with us.
If not these, then others.
We will never know all we wish to know.
Life will always be shrouded in mystery.
Perhaps a goal for us, then, is not to expect answers,
but to expect the unanswerable.
Not to brace ourselves against the mystery,
but to explore what the mystery holds.
For mystery is woven into the living of every one of our days.

*B*ut we cannot stop here.
There is more to mystery than mystery.

> *To see a World in a grain of sand,*
> *And a Heaven in a Wild Flower,*
> *Hold Infinity in the palm of your hand*
> *And Eternity in an hour.*
>
> —William Blake

For those who approach life
  with the widest of eyes and the most open of souls,
    there is in the midst of mystery something more:
      there is a sense of awe.
There is the profound feeling that everything that is around us
  doesn't have to be there.
It makes no sense for it to be there—and yet, there it is!
It astonishes us and baffles us.
We—each of us, all of us—
  have been given the gift of this life, chosen somehow.
This breathing, sensing, dancing life
  has been lavished upon us without our even asking,
    without our even knowing how to ask.
It is beyond our understanding.

When we finally come to realize how extraordinary all this is,
 with our souls as well as with our minds,
  then life begins to change,
   and so do we.
What begins to matter is not just that we've seen and done,
 but how carefully we've seen,
  how thoughtfully we've done.
What matters is not just that we've touched and held,
 but how compassionately we've touched,
  how completely we've held.
What matters is not how many breaths we've taken,
 but how many breaths we've held,
  or that we can hold our breath just now.
What matters is not how much we've known,
 but how much we've loved.
What matters is that the incomprehensible has happened,
 and it continues to happen each moment,
  and it happens to us.

*I*t is not our task to comprehend this.
It is merely our privilege to embrace it.
It is our honor to seize the marvel of this life,
    this day, this moment,
        for what it truly is—precious and sacred.
For clearly imbedded in the mystery surrounding us
    are signs that the One Who Is Far Greater
        is far closer than we could have imagined.
And the promise that the One Who Creates
    is also the One Who Holds.
And the assurance that the One Who Breathes Life
    is also the One Who Brings Hope.

*M*ay you experience that awareness in your life this day.
May you see those signs
    that show you are cared for and loved.
May you hear those promises
    that say your life has unfolding meaning.
May you find in the midst of all the mystery around you,
    if not the experience of wonder,
        then at least the promise of its beginnings.
And may you hold on to that promise.

The Return

*B*y the rivers of Babylon—
　　there we sat down and there we wept
　　　　when we remembered....

　　　　　　　　　　　　　—Psalm 137:1

Our pilgrimage ends where every true pilgrimage ends:
    back where we started.
Back at our own personal experience in life—
    that place we'd rather not be
        yet where we have no choice but to be.
It is a place that can still feel strange and uncomfortable.
Nothing has changed here.
This temporary home of ours still doesn't feel quite like home.
Nothing that happened on the pilgrimage
    altered these surroundings.
Nothing was undone.
And yet, if we look carefully,
    we can see that something has changed.

*T*his place has not changed.
What is different is us.
And that means that everything is somehow different,
  or at least that possibility exists.
If we have entered fully into the pilgrimage experience,
  then the eyes with which we now see
    are not the same eyes we had before.
The ears with which we now hear
  are attuned to new sounds,
    and more subtle ones.
The touch with which we now touch
  is more sensitive than before,
    and more loving.

Who of us enjoys delving more deeply
  into the haunting experience of absence and emptiness?
Who of us is not threatened by unwanted aloneness
  or unwelcome silence?
Who of us does not hesitate
  in the face of the unknown and the unknowable?
Yet the truth is clear:
  facing what we would rather avoid
    can be an enlarging and empowering decision.
There is a strength to be gained in going
  where we do not wish to go.

*B*y choosing to do what is not easy to do
   we come upon a revelation—
      or several revelations.
The first is that all is not as it seems.
Absence, of course, is absence,
   and yet more than absence is there.
There is a rich presence,
   and one particular Presence.
And aloneness can be much more than loneliness.
It can also become a fulfilling solitude,
   as well as an unusual kind of togetherness.
And deep within silence there is something other than silence.
There is an inner voice to be heard,
   and the sound of the spheres,
      and the Word that comes from far beyond.
They all reverberate in harmony.
And hidden within all that is mysterious
   is something far greater than mystery.
There is wisdom beyond simple understanding,
   and there is wonder beyond mere words.

*T*he second revelation is that *we* are not as *we* seem.
We are not who we thought we were.
We are not controlled by the experience of being dislocated.
We are not entirely at its mercy.
We have choices we can make.
We can choose to explore the absence we feel
   in order to see what else waits for us there, expectantly.
We can choose to accept the responsibility of our aloneness
   and discover both the gifts it can offer
     and the company it can provide.
We can choose to linger in the silence
   and to open ourselves to all it communicates.
We can choose to approach the mystery
   and expose ourselves to the magic it can hold.
Whatever our decision, we are freer than we first thought.

*T*he third revelation is that this experience
  of being dislocated and cut off is not as *it* seems either.
Yes, it can hurt.
Yes, it can destroy our plans and our dreams.
Yes, it can rob us of our innocence and our happiness.
But in this far and strange place
  which now seems all too near and all too familiar,
    other forces are at work that we dare not forget.
God is no less present here.
Life is no less real here.
Love is no less true here, and no less possible.
In fact, chances are we will discover through this experience
  what we might not learn in any other way.
We might not know all that we're capable of.
We might not realize all the ways love can embody itself.
We might not experience how healing memories can be,
  or how powerful dreams can be.
We might never know what it feels like to be transformed,
  quietly and unexpectedly.
We might never encounter all the ways life can reassert itself.

*I*n addition to being a place of discomfort,
   this strange land can become in time a place of promise.
In addition to being an assault on our feelings of security,
   this experience of loss can lead us
      to the experience of finding new meaning.
In addition to being a threat,
   this time of dislocation can become a time of blessing
      in a way we could never have expected.
Perhaps not yet,
   perhaps not soon.
But it can happen.
And with courage and hope and perseverance, it will.

*I*n having to go where you least want to go,
   and in choosing to do what is most difficult to do,
      may you discover yourself becoming
         not just a different person
            but a deeper person.
Not just more seasoned,
   but more real.
Not just more knowledgeable,
   but more compassionate.
Not just more hearty,
   but more whole.
May your pilgrimage through your experience of loss
   lead you to both renewed life and replenished hope.
May you come to rediscover what you've never really lost:
   your truest and best self.
And may you arrive at the place where you first started—
   that place which is still the same and yet very different—
      and may you feel this is where you should be.
May you feel like you're coming home.

Other Resources
by James E. Miller

Videos

Grief and Loss

By the Waters of Babylon
A Spiritual Pilgrimage for Those Who Feel Dislocated

Invincible Summer
Returning to Life After Someone You Love Has Died

Listen to Your Sadness
Finding Hope Again After Despair Invades Your Life

How Do I Go On?
Re-designing Your Future After Crisis Has Changed Your Life

We Will Remember
A Meditation for Those Who Live On

Transition

Nothing Is Permanent Except Change
Learning to Manage Transition in Your Life

Spirituality and Healing

Awaken to Hope
Affirming Thoughts to Begin Your Day

Be at Peace
Assuring Thoughts to End Your Day

You Shall Not Be Overcome
Promises and Prayers for Uncertain Times

The Natural Way of Prayer
Being Free to Express What You Feel Deep Within

Caregiving

Grit & Grace of Being a Caregiver
Maintaining Balance as You Care for Others

Spirituality

Common Bushes Afire
Discovering the Sacred in Our Everyday Lives

Why Yellow?
A Quiet Search for That Which Lies Behind All That Is

Older Age

Gaining a Heart of Wisdom
Finding Meaning in the Autumn of Your Life

Books

Grief and Loss

How Can I Help?/What Will Help Me?

When You're Ill or Incapacitated/When You're the Caregiver

Winter Grief/Summer Grace

Older Age

Autumn Wisdom

Audio

The Transforming Potential of Your Grief
Eight Principles for Renewed Life

Willowgreen
P.O. Box 25180
Fort Wayne, Indiana 46825
219/424-7916